TO THE HAPPY COUPLE

to the HAPPY COUPLE

Creating a Great Wedding Toast with Style

BY

SARAH McELWAIN

ILLUSTRATIONS BY

DIANA MARYE

CHRONICLE BOOKS

SAN FRANCISCO

Library of Congress Cataloging-in-Publication Data available.

ISBN 0-8118-4961-9

Manufactured in China.

Designed by AYAKO AKAZAWA

Distributed in Canada by Raincoast Books
9050 Shaughnessy Street
Vancouver, British Columbia V6P 6E5

10 9 8 7 6 5 4 3 2 1

Chronicle Books LLC
85 Second Street
San Francisco, California 94105

www.chroniclebooks.com

TO THE HAPPY COUPLE

AN INTRODUCTION TO WEDDING TOASTS

What would a wedding be without a toast to the health and happiness of the newly married couple? The toast is the time to stand up and celebrate marriage, love, commitment, and the creation of a new family. Some cultures even believe that a marriage that is not properly toasted is jinxed from the start.

Wedding toasts can be traced back to biblical times, and almost every culture has developed its own, often elaborate, form of this tradition. The word "toast" derives from the sixteenth-century French custom of putting bread into the glass before raising it in tribute.

Why is this ancient tradition still an important part of every wedding? In addition to simply marking the occasion, toasts add to the celebratory mood of any wedding. It doesn't matter whether it's a formal affair many months in planning, or a small gathering of friends at a backyard barbecue. A few eloquent, affectionate, or witty toasts will make the occasion more memorable.

Toasts also serve the social function of bringing a room together. At today's weddings, the bride and groom may be from very different ethnic, racial, or class backgrounds, or the couple might be of the same gender. New in-laws are often meeting for the first time. A few well-planned, gracious toasts can help smooth even the most difficult social situation.

Toasts assert our shared values. Love, commitment, and the importance of family, as well as the fun of romance, are the subject of toasts. There may be many differences among the guests at a wedding reception. A good toast reminds all present why they have gathered together on this occasion—to wish love and happiness to the new couple!

There are as many ways to give a wedding toast as there are styles of weddings. A toast can be simple and traditional, as in the classic line, "Here's to love and laughter. . . and happily ever after!" Or a short toast can be proposed with a quotation on love or marriage, such as this selection from Antoine de Saint-Exupéry's well-known work *Le Petit Prince:* "'Love does not consist in gazing at each other but in looking outward together in the same direction.' Here's to Jennifer and Jason!" Alternatively, a longer wedding toast can be a well-composed, beautifully delivered speech that expresses deeper feelings, includes personal anecdotes, and wishes the happy couple well.

Whatever the type of toast, it's important to consider how best to offer it. Who should propose a toast at a wedding and when? What is the difference between a simple toast and a composed toast? How long should a toast be? Part One of *To the Happy Couple* answers these questions and provides guidance on such issues as the role of the best man, toastmaster, or father of the bride; the difference

between good manners and etiquette; and how to serve champagne, a common accompaniment to toasts.

Once you're familiar with the traditions surrounding toasting, it's time to write the perfect toast for your event. Part Two gives simple guidelines for creating just the right toast to fit the mood of the wedding and the personalities of the honorees, with tips on delivering any speech smoothly.

In addition to toasting the health and happiness of the bride and groom, toasts can welcome new in-laws, honor parents, or thank friends and family at any wedding-related event. Part Three of *To the Happy Couple* contains a collection of simple toasts for many occasions. In the "On Love and Marriage" section, you'll find thoughts on wedded love and romance by famous and not-so-famous writers, wits, philosophers, celebrities, and songwriters, all of which can be used as toasts at a wedding reception. If you are looking for a toast to make at a family or rehearsal dinner, the "On Friends and Family" section will provide inspiration. Brides and grooms, too, might want to offer a toast to their new spouses or say a few words thanking family and friends; the "For Brides and Grooms" section is for them.

Sometimes a simple toast is best. If you want to raise your glass and just say "Cheers!" or "To love and luck!" in a language that's appropriate to the bride or groom's heritage, the "In Many Languages" section contains appropriate phrases in everything from Albanian to Zulu.

Toasts are also a part of the fun of pre-wedding festivities. A wickedly irreverent toast can be the highlight of a bachelor party or bridal shower. In "For Bachelor Parties, Bridal Showers, and Jack & Jills" you will find a collection of bawdy, ironic, slightly off-color observations on human behavior and the war between the sexes.

Whatever the theme you choose or the occasion, a heartfelt and appropriate toast is sure to be a treasured part of the memories of the bride and groom, their families, and their guests. Whether you're a bride or groom, a nervous best man giving his first toast, or an experienced master of ceremonies, *To the Happy Couple* is the only guide you'll ever need to create and deliver the perfect wedding toast.

À votre santé!

part ONE

JUST MARRIED
MAY YOU LIVE IN HARMONY AND ALWAYS
THE ULTIMATE TOAST
EVERY WEDDING TOAST ON THE PLANET TO THE REST OF OUR KNOWLEDGE
CONGRATULATIONS
For You
SOMEBODY PLEASE JUST SAVE ME A PIECE OF THAT CAKE BEFORE SHE EATS THE WHOLE THING
I'VE KNOWN THEM BOTH FOR YEARS WELL AT LEAST TWO, THEY ARE MADE FOR EACH OTHER I KNOW BECAUSE I INTRODUCED THEM

PLANNING WEDDING TOASTS

Who should make a wedding toast? And to whom? If you are the best man at a wedding, it's expected that you'll stand up and say a few words about the bride and groom. The maid of honor and the father of the bride are two other members of the traditional wedding party who are often expected to propose a toast.

At formal American weddings, the most traditional order is best man, groom, maid of honor, bride, and the father of the bride. Traditions differ, and at many British weddings the father of the bride normally proposes the first toast, welcoming his guests as the host, whereas the best man closes the party.

These roles can be flexible. The groom's chief attendant may not be a best man in the traditional sense, but his sister or female best friend, and it's perfectly appropriate for her to speak first. Or, if you like, you can ask a family friend or a beloved aunt or uncle to propose a toast. As long as someone stands up and proposes a toast to the health and happiness of the bride and groom, it doesn't really matter who does it.

Anyone who wants to make a wedding toast is usually encouraged to do so. It's easy to get up at a rehearsal dinner or engagement party and propose a toast or to deliver the hilarious speech you've prepared for a bachelor party or bridal shower, thanks to the relative informality of such occasions. But if you want to deliver a personal toast at a wedding reception and are not part of the traditional wedding party, check with the host or planners first. Remember to make sure that no one else delivering a toast at the wedding is planning to use a similar story or the same quotation.

If you are planning a wedding, including such functions as the reception, engagement party, and rehearsal dinner, or hosting a bachelor party or bridal shower, it is fine to delegate the job of making a toast. A good wedding reception requires a lot of behind-the-scenes planning. Knowing who intends to make a toast, what he or she plans to say, and the order in which toasts will be given is essential. Find someone who is practiced at public speaking or speechwriting, or choose a person who you feel might be particularly good at these tasks. The poet in the crowd or a boss, teacher, or friend of the family can always be asked in advance to stand up and lead the rest of the guests in a toast to celebrate the occasion. If the wedding adheres to a traditional format, however, certain members of the wedding party will be expected to speak; here's a guide to their roles.

THE TOASTMASTER

A large or very formal wedding may include a toastmaster or master of ceremonies. The toastmaster or emcee's job is to run the proceedings and keep things going smoothly, much like a cruise director on a luxury liner. The toastmaster's presence allows family members and the wedding party to relax and enjoy the festivities.

In addition to announcing that dinner is about to be served and asking the guests to be seated, the toastmaster also announces the arrival of the bride and groom and escorts them to their places. If a grace or prayer is going to be offered before dinner, the toastmaster introduces the person who will be saying it, usually a family member or the member of the clergy who performed the ceremony. In addition to these duties, the toastmaster also introduces each person who is delivering a toast.

Smaller, less formal weddings may not include a toastmaster, so these tasks can be assigned to various other members of the wedding party. The best man often assumes the role of toastmaster or emcee. If the best man is to do this job successfully, he must be prepared. He needs to have a loud, clear voice, and above all he needs to know the names of everyone he is going to introduce, the order in which he should introduce them, and the approximate times at which events at the reception are supposed to take place.

The toastmaster should . . .

- Make gracious and concise introductions
- Introduce speakers with correct titles
- Learn the proper pronunciation of all names beforehand
- Be prepared to control applause
- Keep an eye on the timing of proceedings; if time becomes a problem, it's fine to start the toasting before all the guests have finished eating
- Prepare appropriate remarks for the end of the reception

THE BEST MAN'S TOAST

At most traditional American wedding receptions, the best man proposes the first toast to the newly married couple. After introducing himself, the best man might begin by congratulating the groom on finding such a wonderful woman. In his speech, he can include a funny anecdote or two about how the couple met, share some of the things the pair has in common, or discuss plans the couple shares for the future. The best man might also mention how important the bride's family is to the groom or use his speech as an opportunity to thank all the guests on behalf of the couple. Sometimes the best man reads messages, cards, e-mails, or faxes from people unable to attend the wedding.

THE GROOM'S TOAST

The groom first responds to the best man's toast by thanking him and then thanks both sets of parents, the bridesmaids and groomsmen, and other friends before saying a few words to the bride. If the bride and groom have written their own vows for the wedding ceremony, then the groom may choose to be brief. If not, he may want to use his toast as an opportunity to talk about how grateful he is to have married such a beautiful and remarkable woman and publicly express his feelings for his new wife.

THE MAID OF HONOR'S TOAST

The maid of honor toasts the bride and groom on behalf of the bridesmaids. She might want to include a personal story about her friendship with the bride, or she might talk about how perfect the bride and groom look together on this special day. Words of advice on love and marriage or a spiritual statement could also be appropriate here, as well as simple good wishes for many years of happiness together.

THE BRIDE'S TOAST

After the maid of honor's toast, the bride may want to toast the groom or thank her family, though she need not speak if she does not wish to do so. If she does speak, she may, like the groom, wish to focus on publicly expressing her love for her new spouse.

THE FATHER OF THE BRIDE'S TOAST

The last toast at a traditional American wedding reception is usually proposed by the father of the bride. He thanks his new son-in-law's family and may want to mention how much he and his wife have enjoyed getting to know them. He can share some personal history about his marriage or family and speak briefly about how proud he is of his daughter. If the bride's parents are hosting the reception, the father of the bride may want to thank all the guests for coming, or he might use his toast as an opportunity to present a special gift to the couple.

TIMING THE TOASTS

At large or formal evening weddings, the toasts usually take place just after dinner, when guests are still seated, and before the cake-cutting ceremony. For less formal and afternoon weddings, or outdoor weddings, the toasts are usually offered after the couple's first dance as husband and wife or at the end of the hors d'oeuvres period, before the cake is cut. Regardless of the timing of the toasts and the size of the reception, it's important to make sure that the caterers, servers, or hosts have poured champagne or another drink for all the guests before toasting begins. Some people believe it's bad luck to toast with an empty glass.

Arranging the toasts at informal or small weddings demands attention to a few extra details. The key issue is to make sure that all the guests are gathered together so that all can be part of the toasting. You'll need to decide whether you want guests to stand or sit, which depends on the timing of the toasts and the events at the reception. If there's no head table, the toasters need to find a place where all the guests can hear the toasts easily. For example, at a small wedding with fourteen guests held at the bride's parents' house, the sister of the bride might make a toast from the fireplace hearth, elevating herself just enough to let people know that she plans to speak and ensuring that all the guests can see and hear her. The toasters or the person planning the reception should check out the venue in advance to determine the best place for gathering guests for toasts.

TIPS ON CHAMPAGNE

"Come quickly, I am tasting stars!"

—DOM PERIGNON, UPON DISCOVERING CHAMPAGNE

CHILL CHAMPAGNE RIGHT

Champagne is always served chilled, never iced. Champagne plunged into a bucket of ice water reaches the right temperature, about 43 to 48°F (6 to 8°C), in 20 to 30 minutes. In a refrigerator, lay the bottles on the bottom shelf for three or four hours before serving.

OPEN THE BOTTLE PROPERLY

First, remove the wire cage from the bottle top. With the cork in your palm, twist the bottle while holding the bottom in your hand until the cork pops out. Many people still think it's great for the cork to fly across the room and for champagne to squirt out all over the place, but this is better suited to events like winning the World Series or the Super Bowl than to weddings. To avoid letting the cork fly—and wasting good champagne—hold a tea towel over the cork.

CHOOSE THE BEST GLASS

Champagne is best served in narrow flutes or tulips. These slender glasses retain the chill of the champagne most effectively and make the bubbles last longer. The thinnest crystal flutes are the glass of choice for champagne drinking. They also make a wonderful wedding present.

KEEP THE FIZZ

Contrary to popular belief, placing a silver spoon in the neck of a champagne bottle doesn't preserve the wine's effervescence. Use a champagne stopper to retain the wine's sparkle after opening.

POUR JUST ENOUGH

Champagne glasses are never poured more than half-full for a toast, especially if many toasts are planned.

OFFER ALTERNATIVES

Champagne is traditionally poured for the toasts at a wedding, but it's essential to have sparkling water or another nonalcoholic beverage, such as sparkling cider or ginger ale, as a readily available alternative at all weddings, no matter how formal or casual.

GIVE CHAMPAGNE AS A GIFT

Instead of a blender, consider writing a special toast for the bride and groom and choosing a bottle of champagne as a wedding present. Nothing expresses how much you care better than a heartfelt short speech delivered in front of friends and family. Add a wonderful bottle of bubbly and you have the perfect gift.

A NOTE ON ALCOHOL

"To alcohol! The cause of, and solution to, all of life's problems!"

—HOMER SIMPSON

It's often a good idea to schedule the toasts early in the festivities. Nobody wants to listen to a best man who has had too many drinks in nervous anticipation of delivering his toast! Also, make sure that food is served before too

many toasts are delivered. Who can forget the groom's parents in *My Big Fat Greek Wedding* getting cross-eyed drunk at the rehearsal dinner when too many toasts with ouzo are made before they have had any food?

Keep in mind, too, that alcohol consumption is forbidden in Muslim countries and by many religious traditions. A great wedding toast can be made with anything: crystal flutes of the finest champagne, paper cups of lemonade, or sparkling water.

THE LENGTH OF TOASTS

Everyone over 30 remembers a wedding toast gone wrong: one that was too long, was too dull, or went on and on. A toast shouldn't run longer than two or three minutes. That amount of time allows you to graciously introduce yourself; say a few personal words, often incorporating a funny anecdote, clever saying, or witty quotation; and conclude with a request to the other guests to join you by raising their glasses and drinking to the health and happiness of the newly married couple.

WHAT'S APPROPRIATE—AND WHAT ISN'T?

In composing a wedding toast, it is important to avoid embarrassing the bride and groom—or, for that matter, anyone in the room. Toasts may be humorous, but should never be mean-spirited. Wedding toasts celebrate love, romance, and commitment—and look to the future. Toasts that refer to former marriages, past disappointments, or mistakes are inappropriate. Always think twice before including information that may not be for general consumption. If you are unsure about whether a particular anecdote is right for the occasion, check with a friend, and remember the golden rule of wedding toasts: When in doubt, leave it out!

When planning a toast, use your judgment to gauge the sensibilities of the guests and the couple. A great toast can contain some pretty irreverent stuff, depending on who is there and if the bride and groom have a good sense of humor. Other difficult subjects can be handled tastefully as well. For instance, it can be meaningful to remember a departed parent: "I know Dad would be so proud of you if he could be here today. . . ." Or referring to a previous relationship might be charming in a groom's toast to his new bride: "We try harder. We're number two!"

Selamat minum!

TRICKY SUBJECTS FOR TOASTS

The following subjects should either be avoided or handled tactfully when composing a wedding toast.

- Previous marriages and relationships
- Recently deceased family members
- Pregnancy
- Losses, disasters, and reversals
- Living together before marriage
- Religious, ethnic, class, or racial differences
- Divorced parents or difficult relationships with in-laws
- Drinking, especially if there may be recovering alcoholics in the audience

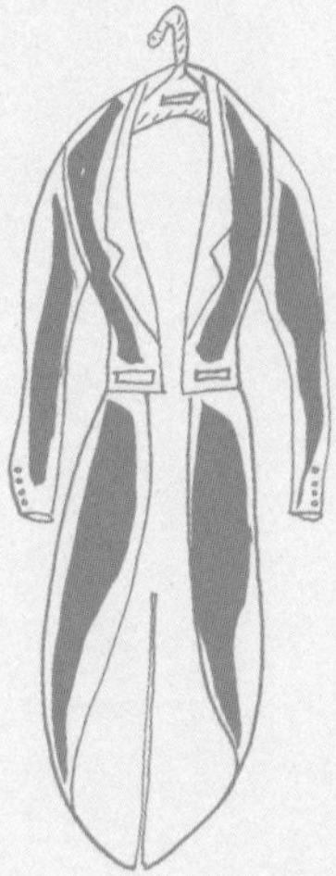

ETIQUETTE VS. GOOD MANNERS

Few social situations are potentially more difficult than a wedding. Cultural sensitivity is often an important issue. The romantic ideal is not accepted as a basis for marriage in every tradition. Guests from some immigrant groups might be uncomfortable making this adjustment. Other cultures have taboos against public displays of affection. When these kinds of issues arise at a wedding, they present a challenge. Understanding the difference between etiquette and good manners can help keep things running smoothly.

Etiquette defines the rules of a cultural group. It covers such matters as which fork to use and how to address people. Like fashion, the rules of etiquette vary from one time or place to another, and they often divide "us" from "them." Manners, on the other hand, promote inclusion. Good manners ensure that no one is made to feel like an outsider by reason of birth, education, or occupation. Manners are concerned with the comfort and ease of everyone in the room.

For example, tying your napkin around your neck instead of holding it in your lap might seem like a breach of etiquette in some cultures. Calling attention to such a lapse would be bad manners. The best solution might be for the host to show good manners by tying his own napkin around his neck to make his guest feel at ease.

The first rule of good manners is to see that everyone feels comfortable. Anything that inconveniences, embarrasses, bores, or denigrates guests is considered bad manners. Using good manners, both in toasting and throughout the event, ensures that no one at a wedding feels excluded or inferior.

OTHER OCCASIONS FOR TOASTS

Weddings are preceded by many festivities, which have an ancient history. Marriage is a rite of passage and for centuries parties have been thrown to celebrate this change of status from single to married. These gatherings also are appropriate occasions for toasts, which can often be different in tone and content from the toasts offered at the wedding itself.

BACHELOR OR STAG PARTIES

Brewer's Dictionary of Phrase and Fable defines a stag party as "a gathering of men only—usually out on a spree." It's a custom that can be traced back to fifth-century Sparta, where soldiers feasted and toasted each other on the eve of a wedding. In later traditions, each man smashed his glass after making his toast so that it could never be used again for a less worthy purpose.

Today, bachelor parties are traditionally the groom's last night out as a single man. Many bachelor parties feature the groom's interests, such as watching a special sporting event or going skiing, bowling, or camping. Bachelor parties can get rowdy and boisterous as the groom celebrates his last taste of freedom; they are often associated with risqué entertainment and excessive drinking. (If this is likely to be the case, it's a good idea to schedule a bachelor party a few days before the wedding ceremony.) Because of the freewheeling, men-only nature of bachelor parties, the toasts offered can be more daring or off-color than what would be expected at a wedding.

BRIDAL SHOWERS

Bridal showers began in the Netherlands in the seventeenth century. There, if a bride's father did not approve of her intended husband and refused to provide her with a

dowry, her friends would give her the presents she needed to bring to the marriage. A more fashionable custom developed later in France, where small gifts were placed in a parasol and opened over or "showered" on the bride's head by her friends and female family members.

Bridal showers have been a traditional way for women of one generation to pass down information and gifts to another and for friends to offer moral support before the big day. A few irreverent toasts can add to the fun: "Here's to men! Give them an inch and they think they're a ruler."

JACK & JILLS

Jack & Jill parties are a more recent invention. Bachelor parties and bridal showers have traditionally kept the sexes separated, but today many couples have pre-wedding parties that include other couples and both of their friends. At such parties, a funny toast can serve as a great icebreaker: "Here's to a happy marriage! It's having breakfast together that causes all the trouble."

Zur Gesundheit und zum Glück!

part TWO

HOW TO COMPOSE AND DELIVER A GREAT WEDDING TOAST

Now you know who does the toasting and why. But what should you actually say? And how should you say it? Begin by thinking about these questions:

First, what is the purpose of your toast? What do you want to express? If this is your best friend's wedding, you might want to compose a speech that honors a long, close friendship. Or is the bride your personal assistant, and the aim of your toast to celebrate her new happiness? Or do you want your toast to entertain? Are you planning to write an irreverent masterpiece to be delivered at a bachelor party or bridal shower?

Whatever your goal, composing a wedding toast provides you with an opportunity to express things you don't get a chance to say every day. Your toast can be your chance to be eloquent, witty, or even mushy! A bride might want to toast her parents by thanking them for their generosity in hosting the wedding. The purpose of the father of the bride's toast is often more practical. It can be a gracious way to welcome new in-laws into the family or to let the guests know that the reception is winding down with a few words of thanks.

Second, who is your audience? When you stand up to deliver your toast, will everyone in the room recognize you, or will you be facing a sea of blank faces? How many guests will be present? If the guests will range widely in age, including small children and great-grandparents, you will need to compose your toast accordingly.

It's important to consider that your toast should be relevant to everyone present. Some guests may not know the bride or groom very well. An anecdote that you and your friends might find funny could be meaningless to other guests or could even seem inappropriate to older family members. Also, if not all the guests speak English, you may want to arrange for a bilingual guest to translate your toast.

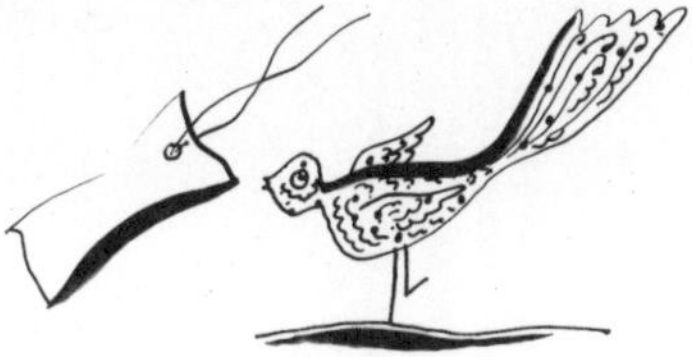

SETTING THE RIGHT TONE FOR YOUR TOAST

As a general rule, the more guests at the wedding reception, the more formal the tone of the toast. A large military wedding or one with hundreds of people in attendance requires more formality than a simple gathering of friends, family, and co-workers. For a very formal occasion, use proper titles such as "the Reverend," "General," or "Doctor" in addressing certain guests or introducing toastmakers. You'll also be expected to address the assembled

guests with such expressions as "ladies and gentlemen" or "honored guests."

The tone of your toast also depends on the style of the couple. Are they elegant and sophisticated or more relaxed and casual? If this is a religious service, the irreverent tone perfect for a theme-park wedding may not go over well. Conversely, a formal toast might not be right for the Elvis Chapel.

COMPOSING A TOAST

A toast is a mini-speech. As most writers will tell you, it takes much more effort to be brief and concise than it does to be long-winded and rambling. Like any speech, a wedding toast should be planned in advance, written down, and then rehearsed so that it can be delivered from memory.

Mark Twain famously said, "It takes three weeks to prepare a good impromptu speech." Don't wait until the last minute! Preparation can make the difference between a beautifully delivered toast and an awkward, tongue-tied moment.

THE RULE OF THREE

Jokes typically have two parts, a set-up and a punch line. Toasts are made up of three parts: the introduction, the tribute, and the request. You can use this formula to compose any kind of toast: a simple, convivial one, or a longer, more personal speech.

USING THE RULE OF THREE TO WRITE A TOAST

1. The Introduction

In the introduction, you simply tell the audience who you are and what your relationship to the person you are toasting is. For example: "I'm__________, and for the past three years I've had the honor of being John's boss."

Don't skip the introduction, even if a toastmaster is introducing you by name. Thank the toastmaster and then explain to the audience who you are: "Angela and I were college roommates, and I flew here last night all the way from Hawaii to help her celebrate this joyous occasion."

At a small, informal wedding, everyone in the room might know you by name, but it is still important to establish your relationship to the person you are toasting. Drag out one of those well-worn family stories: "As you all know, I'm the one who put the fish down Jessica's bathing suit at the beach when she was three." Alternatively, mention something that you're known for: "I'm the one who offered to make my special lasagna when Eddie announced that he was getting married."

2. The Tribute

The tribute is the part of your speech in which you share a personal story or anecdote with the rest of the guests. You can also use the tribute to compliment or honor the person you are toasting. For inspiration, consider these questions and ideas:

How long have you known the bride or groom? How did you meet? What songs did you sing together on the school bus? What is the bride's favorite fairy tale? Did you play "Barbie Gets Married" together? Or were you part of the same winning softball team?

How did the bride and groom meet? Were they partners in a three-legged race at a Fourth of July picnic or

were they in the same litigation and arbitration study group at law school? Were you there when they met, or did you hear about their meeting later?

What interests do the couple share? This question could inspire such tributes as, "When Tina told us that she and Tim went antique hunting together, we knew it was love," or, "In Darlene, Dave has finally found someone who not only listens to his crazy stories about sailing, but who is actually out there with him at five o'clock in the morning on his boat."

How did the groom propose to the bride? Did he rehearse a speech and deliver it over a romantic dinner? Or was it a more spontaneous proposal blurted out in a parking lot after a movie? What was her initial reaction? Did she fly into the office on Monday morning with the big news? Or was the bride the one who did the proposing?

What five words come to mind when you think of the groom? What five words describe the bride? In what ways are they similar? How do they differ? What does each partner bring to the marriage?

Certain toastmakers could include information that sheds light on their distinct role at the wedding. For instance, the maid of honor might want to share the bride's

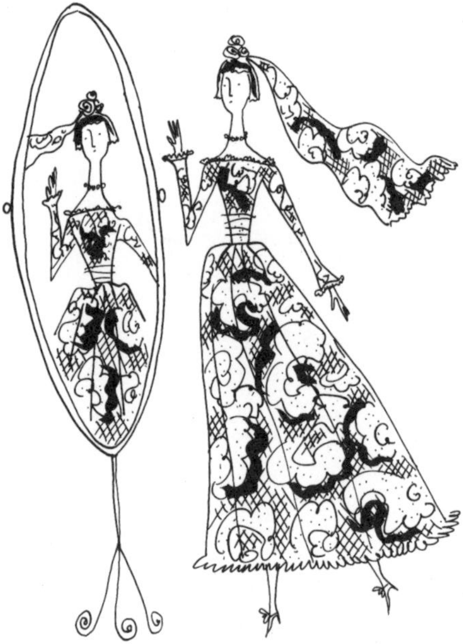

interpretation of "something old, something new, something borrowed, something blue" with the other guests. The father of the bride delivering a toast to his new in-laws at a rehearsal dinner might incorporate a personal memory: "When Jeanette's mother and I visited Tuscany three years ago, we had such a wonderful time. We loved the markets and vineyards, the beauty of the countryside, and the people we met. So you can imagine our great pleasure when Joe's parents turned out to be from Florence!"

If you can find out or remember a toast used at a previous wedding, continue the tradition: "When Grandma and Grandpa got married in 1924, Uncle Louie proposed this traditional Jewish toast: 'Our God has created us a bride and a bridegroom and because of Him we rejoice. May this marriage always be a testimony to His love and providence.' Today, at the wedding of Rebecca and Richard, we wish the two of them the same lasting love and happiness."

3. The Request

After introducing yourself and delivering a short, personal tribute, conclude your toast by requesting that all the guests join you by raising their glasses and drinking in honor of the person or couple being toasted. You can choose a simple and traditional way to make your request, as in the following examples:

"Please raise your glasses as we honor Josh and Jennifer on the joyous occasion of their marriage."

"Here's to Jack and Jackie. We wish you every success in your future and every happiness in your marriage."

"Kevin and Kate, I toast you. May your joys be many and your troubles few, with only success and good health following you."

"Please stand and join me in the traditional toast to the bride and the groom. May the most you wish for be the least you receive."

Alternatively, if you haven't already used a quotation in your tribute, you might choose an appropriate one for the request, as in this example: "I know I speak for everyone here when I say, 'These two are not two. Love has made them one.'" Along similar lines, you could simply borrow from Hugh Grant's character in *Four Weddings and a Funeral*: "To the adorable couple!" Or, incorporate a foreign-language saying such as this Spanish toast: "Amor, salud, dinero, y tiempo para gustarle!" (Love, health, money, and the time to enjoy it!) You'll find many more examples in the "In Many Languages" section in Part Three.

Whatever form your request takes, remember to mention the person or couple you are toasting by name, and then raise your glass and take a sip.

USING QUOTATIONS

You may decide that someone else's words best express what you want to say. Choosing a particularly relevant quotation for the couple or person you are toasting, or one that you feel the other guests might appreciate, can serve as the tribute part of your toast. This might be the time to share some words of wisdom. Is there a quotation you find meaningful? You might begin by quoting 1 Corinthians 13:4–8 from the Bible: "Love is patient; love is kind. . . ." Or you could go in a more irreverent direction: "Whoever said, 'Love is like the measles. The older you get it, the worse the attack,' was probably thinking of Donna and Darryl. . . ."

The father of the bride could begin by paraphrasing Shinichi Suzuki, the Japanese violinist and founder of the Suzuki Method: "They say children learn to smile from their parents. When Jimmy's mother got off the plane, we all saw right away where his big, bright smile came from."

It's also traditional to thank those who have traveled the farthest to attend the wedding. You might begin by quoting comedian George Burns: "Happiness, they say, is having a large, loving, caring, close-knit family in another city. . . ."

You can also use a quotation to evoke a particular person. If the bride and groom are both physicists, for example, you might begin with, "Einstein once observed, 'Gravitation cannot be held responsible for people falling

in love.'" Or, if you know that a large number of the guests are sports fans, you might say: "In the words of basketball coach Phil Jackson, 'Love is the force that ignites the spirit and binds teams together.'"

¡Amor, salud, dinero, y tiempo para gustarle!

SELECTING A POEM OR SHORT READING

Toasts don't need to be original, and an easy way to compose a great toast is to use a short reading or poem. In your tribute, explain briefly why you've chosen this selection for the couple or person you're honoring before you read it. A list of poems and short selections on love and marriage follows. You might want to select just one or two stanzas so you can memorize your reading more easily; print the selection on your index card and use it to refer to. If you do incorporate a poem or reading as part of your toast, you might want to give the couple a copy of the book it comes from as a wedding present. You may also want to ask the couple if they have a favorite poem or reading they would like you to include.

GREAT READINGS FOR TOASTS

The following poems and excerpts can be easily located by typing the title or author's name into an Internet search engine or online library catalog. Most bookstores also carry anthologies devoted to weddings, love, and marriage that may contain many of these selections.

THOMAS À KEMPIS, "*LOVE IS A MIGHTY POWER. . .*"

from The Imitation of Christ, Chapter 42.

THE BUDDHA, "*UNLIMITED FRIENDLINESS*"

from Entering the Stream: An Introduction to the Buddha and His Teachings, by Sherab Chèodzin

SAMUEL TAYLOR COLERIDGE, "*THE PRESENCE OF LOVE*"

E.E. CUMMINGS, "*I CARRY YOUR HEART WITH ME*"

DEBORAH GARRISON, "*SHE WAS WAITING TO BE TOLD*"

KAHLIL GIBRAN, "*LOVE IS A MAGIC RAY,*" from The Prophet

NIKKI GIOVANNI, *SELECTIONS FROM* "*RESIGNATION*"

DONALD HALL, "*VALENTINE*"

LISA JARNOT, "*THEY LOVED THESE THINGS TOO*"

D.H. LAWRENCE, "*FIDELITY*"

MARY OLIVER, "*WEST WIND #2*"

DR. SEUSS, *SELECTIONS FROM OH, THE PLACES YOU'LL GO*

W.B. YEATS, "*A DRINKING SONG*"

INCORPORATE A SONG LYRIC

Who is the couple's favorite songwriter? What was playing the night that they met? Do they have a song? Like poems and other readings, music lyrics can be used creatively in a toast. For example: "The whole office knew something was up with Mario when we heard him singing 'You are the sunshine of my life' at the coffeemaker one morning."

If you're the groom, you may want to begin or end your tribute to your new bride with words borrowed from a song. Let the Temptations say it for you: "You surely must know magic, girl,/ Cause you've changed my life./ It was dull and ordinary/ You made it sunny and bright" (from "You're My Everything"). If the bride and groom don't have a favorite song, dedicate one to them and quote a line or two. "Every time I hear Sarah McLachlan sing 'Wear Your Love Like Heaven,' I think of Matthew and Melissa."

Both CDs and sheet music for popular songs with quotable lyrics are easily available. If you do refer to a song in your toast, make arrangements to have the band play it, or provide the deejay with a copy. Some songs with quotable lyrics are listed on the following pages.

QUOTABLE SONGS

(AND WELL-LOVED PERFORMANCES)

"*ALL MY LIFE*" (LINDA RONSTADT and AARON NEVILLE)

"*ALWAYS MINE*" (SELENA)

"*ANYWHERE FOR YOU*" (BACKSTREET BOYS)

"*A ROOM IN MY HEART*" (FAITH HILL)

"*BECAUSE I LOVE YOU*" (DROP N HARMONY)

"*BECAUSE YOU LOVED ME*" (CELINE DION)

"*BIGGEST PART OF ME*" (AMBROSIA)

"*CAN'T TAKE MY EYES OFF OF YOU*" (FRANKIE VALLI)

"*(EVERYTHING I DO) I DO IT FOR YOU*" (BRYAN ADAMS)

"*FROM THIS MOMENT*" (SHANIA TWAIN)

"*HOW SWEET IT IS (TO BE LOVED BY YOU)*" (MARVIN GAYE and TAMMI TERRELL)

"*I FINALLY FOUND SOMEONE*" (BARBRA STREISAND and BRYAN ADAMS)

"*I KNEW I LOVED YOU*" (SAVAGE GARDEN)

"*I'LL BE THERE*" (MARIAH CAREY)

"*INSEPARABLE*" (NATALIE COLE)

"*IN YOUR EYES*" (PETER GABRIEL)

"*JUST THE WAY YOU ARE*" (BILLY JOEL)

"*LOVE CHANGES EVERYTHING*" (SARAH BRIGHTMAN)

"*ON THE WINGS OF LOVE*" (JEFFREY OSBORNE)

"*SOLID*" (ASHFORD and SIMPSON)

"*STUCK ON YOU*" (LIONEL RICHIE)

"*WHENEVER I CALL YOU FRIEND*" (STEVIE NICKS and KENNY LOGGINS)

"*WITH ARMS WIDE OPEN*" (CREED)

"*YOU'RE THE INSPIRATION*" (CHICAGO)

"*YOUR SONG*" (ELTON JOHN)

GETTING STARTED

Begin by writing a first draft of your toast. In it, you can either write down every word you plan to say or begin with simple notes. For the first draft, don't worry too much about wording or formatting, but do try to keep the tone conversational. Ideally, you will deliver your toast as a speech and make eye contact with guests, rather than reading it with a downcast face. You want your toast to feel spontaneous. With that in mind, remember that the spoken word is different from the written word. When you are writing what you want to say out loud, be sure to use words and phrases that you would use in conversation. For example, contractions such as "it's" and "can't" are more appropriate in a toast than formal forms like "it is" and "cannot." But in your first draft, these details don't matter. What is important is that you get it all down. Write whatever comes to your mind. Don't hold back. There will be plenty of time to edit later.

EDIT YOUR TOAST

Index cards are valuable tools for speechwriting. They help you order and organize your thoughts and are very useful when rehearsing. Once you have a draft you're happy with, edit it into outline form using big type with bullet points. Transfer these key sentences and some talking points onto index cards. Begin with one for your introduction, one or two for your tribute, and one for the request. As you rehearse and become more familiar with your material, you can edit these cards down further.

It's all right to bring these cards with you to the wedding reception, shower, or rehearsal dinner. They come in great colors or can be tucked away discreetly. When you deliver your toast, you will not be reading it, but you can use these cards to refer to. A few signposts or talking points written in big, bold letters can help jog your memory.

PRACTICE, PRACTICE, PRACTICE!

Few people like the idea of standing up in front of a room full of people and delivering a speech, even a short wedding toast. Wedding speeches have an advantage over other kinds of public speaking. They are outwardly directed; that is, they have as their subject someone other than the speaker. Remember, all eyes will be on the person you are toasting, not you.

Rehearsing is the best way to avoid nervousness and to ensure that your toast goes well. Begin by practicing out loud a few times. Underline or boldface words that you want to emphasize in your delivery. After you've become familiar enough with your speech to remember most of it, transfer key sentences and talking points to index cards and practice with a friend. Ask for feedback. Are you emphasizing key words and pausing between sections? The number-one problem in public speaking is talking too fast. Remember to breathe deeply; doing so will slow you down.

WORST-CASE SCENARIO

What happens if, after composing a brilliant, touching toast, you feel too nervous to stand up in front of the audience and deliver it? Don't worry. You can always read from your index cards if you absolutely have to. If you are inexperienced at public speaking or are the type of person whose mind goes blank in front of an audience, you can write your toast down word for word. It is better to share your sentiments with friends and family this way than not at all. Wedding guests are the most forgiving of all audiences.

A FEW DOS AND DON'TS

- Do remember that you will not be reading your toast.
- Don't deliver your toast like your boring history teacher droning over a textbook. You've worked hard to find the right words.
- Do make eye contact with your audience. A toast, like any speech, is a short performance. It's important to look at the person you're honoring and to connect with the other guests.

- Do decide in advance what you are going to do with your hands. Will you place them on a podium? Rest them on the tabletop? Use one hand to hold the back of a chair while the other holds the index cards? Holding the hands awkwardly is a very common problem in public speaking, and knowing what you plan to do in advance will make you look much more at ease.
- Don't forget that rehearsing with a friend will probably feel artificial. Presenting the toast in front of an audience will actually feel much more natural.
- Don't share your toast with too many people. You don't want the whole party to be familiar with it before you stand up.
- Don't rehearse too much. To appear confident you must be completely familiar with your material, but a little nervous excitement is good for public speaking. It raises your energy level and makes you more dynamic. An overly laid-back speaker can be a bore.

- Do be prepared to pause for laughter during certain parts of your toast. Don't try to speak over noise, laughter, or applause. Take a couple of deep breaths while you wait for the audience to quiet down before resuming your toast.
- Do familiarize yourself with the venue, if possible. Gauge how loudly you will have to speak to be heard by all the guests. If you are going to be using a microphone, remember not to speak too closely into it. If possible, test the mike beforehand and make sure you know how to turn it on (and off!).
- Don't call attention to your nervousness or apologize. The disclaimer "Unaccustomed as I am to public speaking. . . " has probably begun more lackluster toasts than any other phrase.
- Don't forget to breathe. A few deep breaths will slow you down and relax you. Nervous speakers tend to talk too quickly.
- Finally, do remember to be yourself. Let your personality come across in your speech. Smile!

REMEMBER, IT'S A PARTY!

It's possible to enjoy the experience of standing up in front of an audience full of friendly faces and making a great wedding toast. You'll feel wonderful when it's over. Your self-confidence will get a huge boost, and you'll get a lot of thanks and praise.

QUICK-REFERENCE TOASTING TIPS

- Unless you are addressing a small, informal group of eight or fewer, stand when making a toast.
- State loudly and clearly that you'd like to propose a toast. The first few words of announcements over loudspeakers often are not heard, especially in large

groups. Begin by saying something like, "Good afternoon, everyone—I'd like to propose a toast."

- When you stand, you should be able to command enough attention to quiet the other guests down.
- Clinking a glass with a knife to quiet a room often ends in broken glass and is generally discouraged. Clinking the glass might also be confused with the informal American tradition of trying to get the newly married couple to kiss.
- If a toastmaster, master of ceremonies, or emcee introduces you, be sure to thank him or her.
- Be sure that everyone has been served champagne or another beverage before you begin.
- At the end of your toast, raise your glass. The person making the toast always takes the first sip. The rest of the guests then follow, raising their glasses,

clinking them if they like, and taking a sip. Clinking glasses before drinking is an ancient toasting tradition. It originated as a way to scare evil spirits away and is still widely practiced today.

- The couple or person being toasted remains seated and neither lifts the glass nor drinks.

Schastya i zdorovya

part THREE

A COLLECTION OF SIMPLE TOASTS

ON LOVE AND MARRIAGE

A good marriage is like a casserole. Only those responsible for it really know what goes into it.

—ANONYMOUS

Here's to the two secrets of a long-lasting and happy marriage: A good sense of humor and a short memory!

—ANONYMOUS

Live this day to the fullest. Remember, it is the first day of the rest of your life.

—ANONYMOUS

Love is like pi—natural, irrational, and very important.

—ANONYMOUS

Love is the only game that is not called on account of darkness.

—ANONYMOUS

Love may not make the world go 'round,
but it sure makes the trip worthwhile!

—ANONYMOUS

Marriage is the triumph of imagination over intelligence.
Second marriage is the triumph of hope over experience.

—ANONYMOUS

May this union be one that never goes on strike!

—ANONYMOUS

Success is getting what you want,
Happiness is liking what you get.

—ANONYMOUS

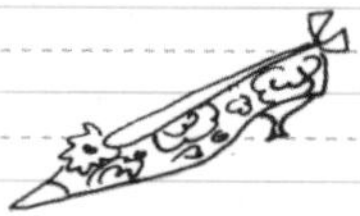

You will find that two can't live as cheaply as one,
but it's well worth the difference.

—ANONYMOUS

May you be shelter to each other.
May you be warmth to each other.
May your days be long and good upon this earth.

—APACHE WEDDING PRAYER

A successful marriage requires falling in love over and over with the same person.

—APHORISM

Life is so much better when it is shared.

—APHORISM

Loving someone is like caring for a garden: Love it too much or too little and it dies, but love it just right and it will live forever.

—APHORISM

The greatest thing about love is that you know when it is here.

—APHORISM

The most important part of the pursuit of happiness is choosing the right traveling companion.

—APHORISM

To the world you might be one person,
But to one person you might be the world.

—APHORISM

We come to love not by finding a perfect person, but by learning to see an imperfect person perfectly.

—APHORISM

You are never too young to fall in love,
And never too old to wish you had.

—APHORISM

You don't marry someone you can live with; you marry the person whom you cannot live without.

—APHORISM

May you grow old on one pillow.

—ARMENIAN WEDDING BLESSING

Love, be true to her,
Life, be dear to her,
Health, stay close to her,
Joy, draw near to her,
Fortune, find what you can do for her,
Search your treasure house through for her,
Follow her footsteps the wide world over,
And keep her husband always her lover.

—ENGLISH TOAST

May the road you travel together be filled with
much love and success!

—IRISH WEDDING BLESSING

A marriage without a sense of humor is like a wagon
without springs—jolted by every pebble in the road.

—ITALIAN PROVERB

Our God has created us a bride and a bridegroom and because of Him we rejoice. May this marriage always be a testimony to His love and providence.

—JEWISH TOAST

The heart knows when the search is over.

—PROVERB

A life without love is like a year without summer.

—PROVERB

Love is in the giver, not the gift.

—PROVERB

True love doesn't have a happy ending;
true love doesn't have an ending.

—PROVERB

Where love is concerned, too much is never enough.

—PROVERB

[Bride] and [groom], we toast you.
May you always be as happy as you are today.

—TRADITIONAL TOAST

Here's to love, laughter,
And happily ever after.
As [the groom] and [the bride] start their new life,
Let's toast the new husband and wife!

—TRADITIONAL TOAST

Here's to the new husband,
And here's to the new wife.
May they remain lovers
Every day of their lives.

—TRADITIONAL TOAST

Let us drink to love, which is nothing—
unless it's divided by two.

—TRADITIONAL TOAST

To [the groom], the luckiest man on earth.
And [the bride], the woman who made him that way.

—TRADITIONAL TOAST

With love to you on your day of days
We lift our glasses to sing your praise.

—TRADITIONAL TOAST

May the young couple be as rich as the earth!

—WEDDING BLESSING

May you be friends to each other as only lovers can.
May you love each other as only best friends can.

—WEDDING BLESSING

May you find the serenity of oneness.

—WEDDING BLESSING

May your fire never go out!

—WEDDING BLESSING

May your marriage be like this fine wine,
growing better and better with age.
To [the bride] and [the groom]:
Welcome to the next chapter of your life.

—WEDDING BLESSING

These two are not two; love has made them one.

—WEDDING BLESSING

Love is patient;
love is kind;
love is not envious or boastful or arrogant or rude.
It does not insist on its own way;
it is not irritable or resentful;
it does not rejoice in wrongdoing,
but rejoices in the truth.
It bears all things, believes all things,
hopes all things, endures all things.
Love never ends.

—I CORINTHIANS 13:4–8

If it is your time, love will track you down like a cruise missile.

—CARTOONIST LYNDA BARRY

In our life there is a single color, as on an artist's palette, which provides the meaning of life and art. It is the color of love.

—RUSSIAN ARTIST MARC CHAGALL

Love can make you do things that you never thought possible!

—SINGER-SONGWRITER PHIL COLLINS

It takes a smart woman to fall in love with a good man.

—WRITERS SADIE AND BESSIE DELANY, *HAVING OUR SAY*

That love is all there is,
Is all we know of Love.

—POET EMILY DICKINSON, "THAT LOVE IS ALL THERE IS"

Cool breeze. Warm fire.
Full moon. Easy chair.
Empty plates. Soft words.
Sweet songs. Tall tales.
Short sips. Long life.

—SOUTHERN WRITER JOHN EGERTON

Gravitation cannot be held responsible
for people falling in love.

—NOBEL PRIZE–WINNING THEORETICAL PHYSICIST ALBERT EINSTEIN

Nobody has ever measured, not even poets,
how much the heart can hold.

—WRITER ZELDA FITZGERALD

Anyone can be passionate,
but it takes real lovers to be silly.

—PLAYWRIGHT ROSE FRANKEN

Life without love is like a tree without blossoms or fruit.

—POET KAHLIL GIBRAN, *THE PROPHET*

We love because it's the only true adventure.

—POET NIKKI GIOVANNI

The time to be happy is now;
the place to be happy is here.

—AMERICAN ORATOR ROBERT INGERSOLL

Love is the force that ignites the spirit and binds teams together.

—BASKETBALL COACH PHIL JACKSON, *SACRED HOOPS*

The meeting of two personalities is like
the contact of two chemical substances;
if there is any reaction,
both are transformed.

—PSYCHOLOGIST CARL JUNG

People think love is an emotion. Love is good sense.

—AUTHOR KEN KESEY

Love bravely, live bravely, be courageous,
there's really nothing to lose.

—SINGER-SONGWRITER JEWEL KILCHER

You must always be a-waggle with love.

—NOVELIST AND POET D.H. LAWRENCE, "BIBBLES"

Love one another and you will be happy. It's as simple
and as difficult as that.

—AUSTRALIAN CARTOONIST MICHAEL LEUNIG

Age does not protect us from love, but love to some extent
protects us from age.

—FRENCH FILM STAR JEANNE MOREAU

Love is or it ain't. Thin love ain't love at all.

—NOVELIST TONI MORRISON, *BELOVED*

A good marriage is based on a talent for friendship.

—GERMAN PHILOSOPHER FRIEDRICH NIETZSCHE, *HUMAN, ALL TOO HUMAN*

Love is like the measles. The older you get it, the worse the attack.

—MYSTERY WRITER MARY ROBERTS RHINEHART

Love is a little haven of refuge from the world.

—BRITISH PHILOSOPHER BERTRAND RUSSELL

Love does not consist in gazing at each other, but in looking outward together in the same direction.

—FRENCH WRITER ANTOINE DE SAINT-EXUPÉRY, *LE PETIT PRINCE*

Love is friendship set on fire.

—THEOLOGIAN JEREMY TAYLOR

There is no remedy for love but to love more.

—AMERICAN WRITER AND PHILOSOPHER HENRY DAVID THOREAU

Love has no awareness of merit or demerit;
it has no scale by which its portion may be
weighed or measured.
It does not seek to balance by giving and receiving.
Love loves; this is its nature.

—MINISTER AND CIVIL RIGHTS LEADER HOWARD THURMAN

Love is being stupid together.

—FRENCH SYMBOLIST POET PAUL VALÉRY

Love is the same as like except you feel sexier.

—AUTHOR JUDITH VIORST

I have learned not to worry about love;
But to honor its coming with all my heart.

—POET AND NOVELIST ALICE WALKER, "NEW FACE"

Who, being loved, is poor?

—POET AND PLAYWRIGHT OSCAR WILDE,
A WOMAN OF NO IMPORTANCE

Love is what you go through together.

—PLAYWRIGHT THORNTON WILDER

FOR BRIDES AND GROOMS

Because I love you truly,
Because you love me, too,
My very greatest happiness
Is sharing life with you.
Every day you look lovelier and lovelier,
and today you look like tomorrow.

—ANONYMOUS

Come live in my heart, and pay no rent.

—ANONYMOUS

If I know what love is, it is because of you.

—ANONYMOUS

I love the sun for days,
the moon for nights, and you forever!

—ANONYMOUS

I love you more than yesterday and less than tomorrow.

—ANONYMOUS

I love you not only for what you are, but for what I am when I am with you.

—ANONYMOUS

I love you simply because I cannot help it. Here's to you!

—ANONYMOUS

May our love be perfect, even if we are not.

—ANONYMOUS

My love for you is a journey,
starting at forever, and ending at never.

—ANONYMOUS

Never above you.
Never below you.
Always beside you.

—ANONYMOUS

Once upon a time, on a day like any other, someone like no other came along and made my life into something that would never be the same.

—ANONYMOUS

Sometimes I wonder if love is worth fighting for,
But then I remember your face and I'm ready for war.

—ANONYMOUS

To my husband, together, forever, down life's long road.

—BRIDE'S TOAST

You are my reason to run, to dance, to think, to see.
Most of all you are my reason to love.

—ESKIMO WEDDING PRAYER

Here's to my bride, who knows everything about me,
yet loves me just the same.

—GROOM'S TOAST

To my bride,
Today our dreams come true.
Here's to you!

—GROOM'S TOAST

To my wife, my bride and joy.

—GROOM'S TOAST

To my wife: We've only just begun.

—GROOM'S TOAST

To [the bride], my inspiration,
My light, my love.

—GROOM'S TOAST

In me is nothing mine
In me are all things yours
I give you what is yours
And do not lose what's mine.

—INDIAN DOHA-A

A part of you has grown in me.
And so you see, it's you and me
Together forever and never apart,
Maybe in distance, but never in heart.

—POETIC TOAST

Here's to my best friend.
I'd do anything for you.
Let nothing come between us.
My love is strong and true.

—POETIC TOAST

I have known many,
Liked not a few,
Loved only one,
I drink to you.

—POETIC TOAST

Love is being with you,
Saying I love you too,
Love is your tender kiss,
Something I don't want to miss,
Love is you and me,
And that is all I see.

—POETIC TOAST

There are lots of things
With which I'm blessed,
But of all my blessings,
This one's the best:
To have a friend like you.

—POETIC TOAST

Grow old along with me.

The best is yet to be.

—ENGLISH POET ROBERT BROWNING, "RABBI BEN EZRA"

You made my jagged edges smooth.

—POP GROUP THE COMMODORES, "JUST TO BE CLOSE TO YOU"

I'll let you be in my dreams, if I can be in yours.

—SINGER-SONGWRITER BOB DYLAN, "TALKIN' WORLD WAR III BLUES"

You cheer my life with every smile.

—BLACK NATIONALIST MARCUS GARVEY, "LOVE'S MORNING STAR"

For all that has been—thanks!

For all that will be—yes!

—FORMER UNITED NATIONS SECRETARY-GENERAL DAG HAMMARSKJÖLD

You are the gift of love to me.

—EVELYN MARIA HARRIS, MEMBER OF SWEET HONEY IN THE ROCK,

"GIFT OF LOVE"

If you fall, I will catch you—I'll be waiting,

Time after time.

—SINGER-SONGWRITER CYNDI LAUPER, "TIME AFTER TIME"

I never thought I could ever really love anything without

four wheels and a stick shift.

—MICHAEL MACFARLANE

You are my shining star!

—POP GROUP THE MANHATTANS, "SHINING STAR"

Came but for friendship and took away love.

—IRISH POET THOMAS MOORE

I love you. And it's getting worse.

—AUTHOR JOSEPH MORRIS, *IT CAN BE DONE: POEMS OF INSPIRATION*

Take my hand, take my whole life too
For I can't help falling in love with you.

—SINGER ELVIS PRESLEY, "CAN'T HELP FALLING IN LOVE"

Deep in my heart
How the presence of you shines
In a light to last a whole life through.

—SINGER-SONGWRITER PATTI SMITH, "DREAM OF LIFE"

This is my beloved and this is my friend.

—SONG OF SOLOMON 5:16

I seem to have loved you in numberless forms,
numberless times,
In life after life, in age after age, forever.

—BENGALI POET RABINDRANATH TAGORE, "UNENDING LOVE"

ON FRIENDS AND FAMILY

Here's to my mother-in-law's daughter,
Here's to her father-in-law's son;
Here's to the vows we've just taken,
And the life we've just begun.

—ANONYMOUS

It is written: when children find true love,
parents find true joy.
Here's to your joy and ours, from this day forward.

—ANONYMOUS

The Lord gives us our relatives.
Thank God we can choose our friends!

—ANONYMOUS

To all the memories we have shared and
the new ones we are creating.

—ANONYMOUS

To my best friend's new best friend!

—ANONYMOUS

Marriage is like a cultural handrail. It links us to the past and guides us to the future.

—APHORISM

There's so much friendship in love,
And so much love in friendship,
It's impossible to know where friendship ends
and love begins.

—APHORISM

The goodness of the father reaches higher than a mountain; that of the mother goes deeper than the ocean.

—JAPANESE PROVERB

Good fathers make good sons.

—PROVERB

The most meaningful gift a father gives to his children
is to love their mother.

—PROVERB

Treat your family like friends and your friends like family.

—PROVERB

A tree is known by its fruit.

—PROVERB

May our house always be too small to hold
all of our friends.

—TRADITIONAL BLESSING

Here's a toast to the future,
A toast to the past,
A toast to our friends,
May our love ever last.

—TRADITIONAL TOAST

May your troubles be less
And your blessings be more
And nothing but happiness
Come through your door.

—TRADITIONAL TOAST

To the bridesmaids: Thank you for adding beauty to this special day.

—TRADITIONAL TOAST

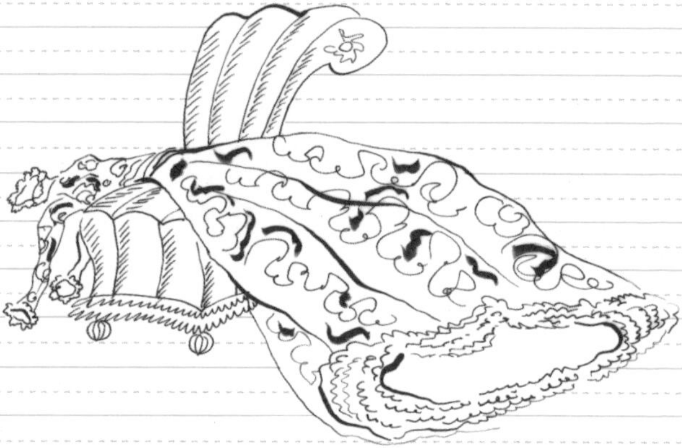

To the grandparents!
Let us raise our glasses
And then imbibe
To the splendid couple
Who founded this tribe.

—TRADITIONAL TOAST

Grandchildren are God's way of compensating us for growing old.

—YIDDISH SAYING

There are only two lasting bequests we can hope to give our children. One of these is roots, the other wings.

—AUTHOR HODDING CARTER

No matter what you've done for yourself or for humanity,
if you can't look back on having given love and
attention to your own family,
what have you really accomplished?

—FORMER CHRYSLER CHAIRMAN LEE IACOCCA

Some friends come and some friends go
But you are the truest friend I know.

—AMERICAN HOSTESS AND GOSSIP COLUMNIST ELSA MAXWELL

What is a family, after all, except memories?
Haphazard and precious as the contents of a catch-all
drawer in the kitchen.

—AUTHOR JOYCE CAROL OATES

Family isn't about whose blood you have.
It's about who you care about.

—TELEVISION WRITERS TREY PARKER AND MATT STONE, *SOUTH PARK*

This is the day that the Lord has made;
let us rejoice and be glad in it.

—PSALM 118:24

Children learn to smile from their parents.

—JAPANESE VIOLINIST SHINICHI SUZUKI

IN MANY LANGUAGES

SPELLINGS AND TRANSLATIONS ARE APPROXIMATE.

Gëzuar!

[GUH-zuh-ar]

(Cheers!)

—ALBANIAN TOAST

Gan bei!

[gahn bay]

(Dry the cup!)

—CHINESE (MANDARIN) TOAST

Liefde en Geluk!

[LEEV-deh en jeh-LUCK]

(Love and happiness!)

—DUTCH TOAST

Bisochtak!

[bee-SOTCH-tack]

(Cheers!)

—EGYPTIAN TOAST

Je via sano!

[YEH VEE-ah SAH-no]

(To your health!)

—ESPERANTO TOAST

Å votre santé!

[ah VO-truh SAHN-tay]

(To your health!)

—FRENCH WEDDING TOAST

Zur Gesundheit und zum Glück!

[zoor geh-ZOOND-hite oond zoom GLUCK]

(To health and happiness!)

—GERMAN WEDDING TOAST

Jamas!

[YAH-mass]

(Cheers!)

—GREEK TOAST

Okole maluna!

[AH KAH-lay mah-LOO-nah]

(Cheers!)

—HAWAIIAN TOAST

L'chaim!

[leh KHAY-im]

(To life!)

—HEBREW WEDDING TOAST

Sok boldogaságot!

[sok bold-og-as-agot]

(Lots of happiness!)

—HUNGARIAN TOAST

Selamat minum!

[SUH-lah-mat mi-noom]

(Cheers!)

—INDONESIAN TOAST

Slàinte!

[SLAWN-cha]

(To health!)

—IRISH (GAELIC) TOAST

Cent' anni!

[chent AHN-nee]

(To one hundred years!)

—ITALIAN TOAST

Kanpai!

[KAN-pi]

(Cheers! / Dry the cup)

—JAPANESE TOAST

Salutem!

[sah-LOOT-em]

(Cheers!)

—LATIN TOAST

I sveikata!

[ee svayk-AHT-ah]

(Cheers!)

—LITHUANIAN TOAST

Kia ora!

[KEE-ah OH-ra]

(Stay well!)

—MAORI TOAST

Elsk og lykke!

[elsk oog LICK-uh]

(Love and happiness!)

—NORWEGIAN TOAST

Nush!

[noosh]

(Enjoy it, and let it be part of your body!)

—IRANIAN (FARCI) TOAST

Na zdrowie!

[nah zuh-DRO-vyeh]

(Here's to your health!)

—POLISH TOAST

Amor e felicidade!

[ah-MORE ay fay-lee-see-DAHD-ay]

(Love and happiness!)

—PORTUGUESE TOAST

Noroc!

[noh-RAHK]

(Good luck!)

—ROMANIAN TOAST

Schastya i zdorovya!

[SHAST-ya ee zuh-dor-OH-wa]

(I wish you happiness and health!)

—RUSSIAN TOAST

Alles van de bestor!

[AHL-es vahn deh BEST-or]

(All the best!)

—AFRIKAANS (SOUTH AFRICAN) TOAST

¡Amor, salud, dinero, y tiempo para gustarle!

[ah-MORE, sah-LOOD, dee-NAYR-oh,

ee tee-EM-po PAH-rah goo-STAR-lay]

(Love, health, money, and the time to enjoy it!)

—SPANISH TOAST

Skal!

[skahl]

(Cheers!)

—SWEDISH TOAST

Mabuhay!

[mah-BOO-high]

(Long life!)

—TAGALOG TOAST

Chia!

[jee-ah]

(Cheers!)

—VIETNAMESE TOAST

Oogy wawa!

[oo-gee wa-wa]

(Cheers!)

—ZULU TOAST

FOR BACHELOR PARTIES, BRIDAL SHOWERS, AND JACK & JILLS

Be bold in what you stand for
And careful what you fall for.

—ANONYMOUS

Everyone has two husbands: the one she is given,
and the one she creates.

—ANONYMOUS

Here's to marriage! For a man is not complete until
he is married, and then he is finished.

—ANONYMOUS

Love may be blind, but it can sure find its way
around in the dark!

—ANONYMOUS

Marriages are all happy. It's having breakfast together that causes all the trouble.

—ANONYMOUS

May your life be long and sunny,
And your husband fat and funny!

—ANONYMOUS

There are two theories about arguing with a woman. Neither one works.

—ANONYMOUS

To marriage—the only war in which you sleep with the enemy.

—ANONYMOUS

To marriage, which is made in heaven—
but don't forget, so are thunder and lightning.

—ANONYMOUS

To men: Give them an inch,
and they think they're a ruler.

—ANONYMOUS

To the men I've loved
To the men I've kissed
My heartfelt apologies
To the men I've missed!

—ANONYMOUS

Women's faults are many,
Men have only two:
Everything they say
And everything they do!

—ANONYMOUS

Marriage has teeth, and him bit very hard.

—JAMAICAN PROVERB

Love is an exploding cigar that we willingly smoke.

—CARTOONIST LYNDA BARRY

Let us now set forth one of the fundamental truths about marriage—the wife is in charge.

—COMEDIAN AND ACTOR BILL COSBY

My wife and I were happy for twenty years. Then we met.

—COMEDIAN AND ACTOR RODNEY DANGERFIELD

Never go to bed mad. Stay up and fight.

—COMEDIAN AND ACTOR PHYLLIS DILLER

Love is a perky elf dancing a merry little jig, and then suddenly he turns on you with a miniature machine gun.

—CARTOONIST AND *THE SIMPSONS* CREATOR MATT GROENING, "LIFE IN HELL"

Women should be obscene and not heard.

—SINGER-SONGWRITER JOHN LENNON

Wives are people who feel they don't dance enough.

—COMEDIAN AND ACTOR GROUCHO MARX

A husband is a guy who tells you when you've got on too much lipstick and helps you with your girdle when your hips stick.

—POET OGDEN NASH

Always get married early in the morning. That way, if it doesn't work out, you haven't wasted a whole day.

—EIGHT-TIMES-MARRIED ACTOR MICKEY ROONEY

I think men who have a pierced ear are better prepared for marriage—they've experienced pain and bought jewelry.

—WRITER AND COMEDIAN RITA RUDNER

If love is the answer, could you rephrase the question?

—COMEDIAN AND ACTOR LILY TOMLIN

SARAH McELWAIN is the editor of *Saying Grace: Blessings for the Family Table* and @METRO, The Metropolitan New York Library Council Newsletter. She lives in New York City and teaches at The Writers Studio.

DIANA MARYE is a writer and illustrator who moved from New York to California to give her two cats a better view. She is currently working on a book about the painter Toulouse-Lautrec.